KU-344-417

Pirate Treasure

written by
Tytus Huffman

illustrated by
Peter Dennis

Guildtown Primary School
Perthshire

PERTH & KINROSS
EDUC. DEPT.

00038

38

Macdonald Educational

There old Kidd lies with his staring eyes,
Looking out to the Westward-ho!
And none can tell where his treasure dwells,
On isle or down below-ho!

In the eighteenth century this was just one of the songs sung about Captain William Kidd and his buried treasure. Many people did more than just sing songs about the old pirate's loot. They looked high and low for it.

In America they searched along the eastern coast. The treasure hunters sank shafts in the rivers that flowed into the Atlantic. They pockmarked the islands off the city of New York with their diggings and scoured the green West Indies in their search. Sailors' sea chests were closely examined for secret compartments that might hold gold coins or treasure maps. The memories of old sailors were jogged to see if they could remember Captain Kidd's visit to their shores.

For you see there could be no help
from Kidd himself.

In 1701 the captain was hung at
Execution Dock in Wapping for murder
and piracy on the high seas. The people
that backed his voyages of piracy chose
to sacrifice him to save themselves. And
so Kidd's body swung in irons while
three tides swept beneath it. Spectators
came to stare at the famous pirate.

Before his execution, while Kidd was in jail, he had offered to lead his captors to a great treasure in Haiti. He said it was worth £100,000, a fortune then. But he wasn't allowed to leave prison.

Certain facts were known about Kidd's voyage. He sailed to the Indian Ocean in 1697. His ship was called the *Adventure*. Near the island of Madagascar he captured two great treasure ships called the *Quedah Merchant* and the *Rouparelle*. They belonged to the Grand Mogul of India. In the ships' holds were bars of gold and silver, cornelian rings, agates and amethysts, silver buttons, silk cloth striped with threads of gold, bags of jaspar, bales of cotton and beautifully lacquered furniture.

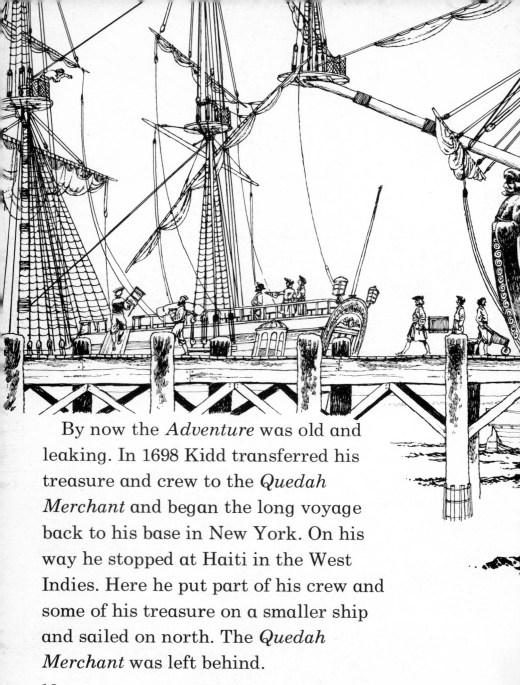

By now the *Adventure* was old and leaking. In 1698 Kidd transferred his treasure and crew to the *Quedah Merchant* and began the long voyage back to his base in New York. On his way he stopped at Haiti in the West Indies. Here he put part of his crew and some of his treasure on a smaller ship and sailed on north. The *Quedah Merchant* was left behind.

10

No sooner was Kidd out of sight than his sailors shared the loot left on the *Quedah Merchant*. They burnt the ship to the waterline and they disappeared into the island. The sailors sold the bales of cotton and silk to local merchants. They buried the gold, silver and precious stones. They bribed the local governor with the rest of the treasure and he let them live in peace on the island. Many of the pirates married and grew rich. Some of the treasure was hidden in their homes. Other treasure was buried and secret maps drawn.

Many years later, during the great slave rebellion in Haiti, fire and war swept the island. The pirates' treasure was stolen from the ruins of the burnt houses. The secret maps were burnt to ashes.

Early in 1699 Kidd was sailing off th
American coast. He left treasure
wherever he anchored on the way
north. Some of the treasure he left at
the mouths of rivers. It seemed Kidd
also left some of his treasure near New
York.

Two of his crew were captured in
New Jersey and Pennsylvania. On these
men and in the sea chests their horses
carried, officials found thousands of
pieces of eight, Arabian gold, coral
necklaces and bales of Indian silk.

Another sailor, armed to the teeth, was seen rowing ashore from the pirate ship. When he landed he lifted two chests onto his shoulders, strode past the people on the beach and vanished in the forest beyond. No one dared stop him.

In early June Kidd's ship dropped anchor at Nassau, Long Island. A smaller ship drew alongside. On her was Kidd's old quartermaster. For three days people on the shore watched as the quartermaster transferred chests and bales from the larger ship to his own ship. On the third night he sailed quietly away.

Kidd's last anchorage on his journey to New York was Gardiner's Island. Here he gave bags of gold and silver dust to the island's owner. The wife received a gold cloth. Everyone who came aboard the pirate vessel went away laden with gifts. Even the man Kidd chose to deliver a message to his backer in New York, was given a gilded box studded with jewels. Inside the box were five bags of gold and a handkerchief laced with strands of silver.

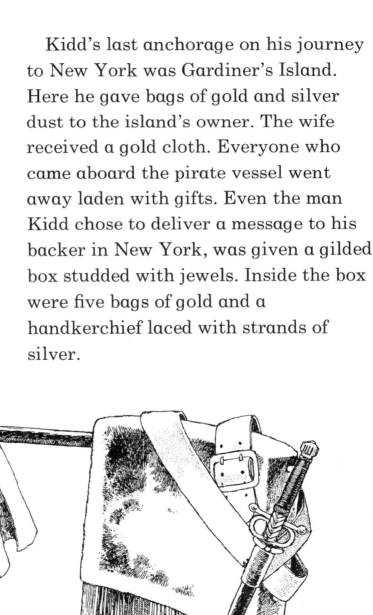

When Kidd's ship was finally unloaded in New York in July the value of the goods on it was £14,000. But there must have been some treasure overlooked for many poor islanders were seen to have new fishing boats or were building new homes.

By now hungry treasure hunters were listening to any clues whatsoever. People up the Hudson River remembered a tall ship sailing by. It anchored near Polypus Island. There was a great fire one night and next morning only the blackened hull remained. The crew had vanished. Later an old sailor came to the nearby village, He spoke of buried treasure and asked for help in digging it up. No one went with him. Several days later the seaman returned. He bought a quantity of goods with an assortment of foreign coins. Then he purchased a boat and rowed down to the sea.

Too late the villagers realised what they had missed. An expedition to the site of the sunken ship was able to locate it. All they recovered from the mud-covered wreck was a few rusty flintlock pistols and a brass cannon.

On Block Island, Kidd's Island,
Martha's Vinyard and Long Island, all
near New York, the land was pitted by
treasure hunters. People dived in
Tarpolin Cove, Oyster Bay and the
'Money Pond', yet only on Martha's
Vinyard were any valuables recovered.
A farmer there ploughed up 1800 dollars
worth of Spanish coins called reals.

Pirate legend always spoke of a
midnight burial of Kidd's treasure with
the captain and two men landing on a
silent shore. While Kidd held his
lantern high his two henchmen dug a
hole in the sand. After the loot was
buried there was a pistol shot. Then two
men rowed back to Kidd's waiting ship.

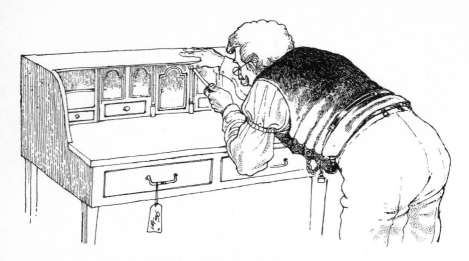

Thirty years after the American Revolution there was a very high tide on the beach near Newport, Rhode Island. The waves washed out a skeleton from the sand. Old people there recalled tales from their youth of a man buried on the beach to guard a nearby treasure. But no pirate hoard was found.

Much later an old seaman's chest, a desk and a ship's table, all believed to be Kidd's, found their way into an antique shop. They were examined closely and secret compartments discovered in them.

Inside the drawers were identical maps of an island. Written on each of them in lettering typical of the seventeenth century, were the words 'Skeleton Island'. From the latitude given and the shape of the island the place was thought to be in the Indian Ocean, Kidd's old haunt. But in those days sailors couldn't measure longitude very well with their simple navigation instruments. This vital direction was missing on all the maps.

Perhaps the maps were fake after all, drawn up by the antique dealer. Perhaps, as many authorities said, there was no Captain Kidd's treasure buried in some secret place. Maybe most of it really was recovered by Kidd's backer in New York, stolen by his men or given away by the pirate himself.

If that is true then it is only a mirage, a daydream, that people searched for all those years. It was just Captain Kidd's pot of gold 'neath the rainbow, something no one would ever find because there was nothing to find.

But after all those years how can anyone be certain? Whether or not there is a Captain Kidd's buried treasure is still a riddle.

Other Macdonald Adventures are:
To the South Pole
Voyage of the Kon-Tiki
The Great Escaper
Battle of the Alamo
Lawrence of Arabia

Macdonald Adventures to be published are:
Curse of the Pharoahs
Ascent of Everest
The Search for Livingstone
Escape across the Mountains
The Wright Brothers
The Indian Princess